What the New Testament Says About Holiness

J. Harold Greenlee

ISBN 0-88019-326-3

Schmul Publishing Co., Inc.
Wesleyan Book Club   Salem, Ohio
1994

ABOUT THE AUTHOR

J. Harold Greenlee: A.B., Asbury College; B.D., Asbury Theological Seminary; M.A. in Ancient Languages, University of Kentucky; Ph.D. in Biblical and Patristic Greek, Harvard University; Senior Fulbright Fellow, Oxford University. He is a missionary of OMS International and an international Greek consultant for Wycliffe Bible Translators/Summer Institute of Linguistics. He was formerly Professor of New Testament Greek in Asbury Theological Seminary. He is the author of many articles and several books dealing with the Greek New Testament; his *Concise Exegetical Grammar Of New Testament Greek* has been issued in seven languages. He is an ordained United Methodist minister.

Printed by
Old Paths Tract Society, Inc.
Route 2, Box 43
Shoals, Indiana 47581

TABLE OF CONTENTS

PREFACE

Holiness is at the very heart of the Christian faith. Holiness describes the normal Christian life. The life of holiness has been dealt with in a very practical and helpful way by numerous authors. I want to recommend two of these. One is *The Christian's Secret of a Happy Life*, by Hannah Whitall Smith, written a century ago in simple Quaker style and probably never out of print since then. The other is Ken Abraham's recent book, *Positive Holiness*. Both of these books are published by Revell, the former being one of that publisher's earliest publications.

Preachers and writers, in dealing with this important subject, refer of course to passages of Scripture, sometimes with conflicting interpretations. I have therefore felt that a careful study was needed that deals with the actual words in the original language of the New Testament—words which are translated into English by such words as *holy, holiness, sanctify, sanctification,* and *saints*. This little booklet is my effort to meet that need. I commend it to all who want to know what these New Testament words actually tell us about Christian holiness.

The New Testament passages which I quote are my own translation of the Greek text, and the Old Testament quotations are from the NIV, unless otherwise noted.

Chapter 1

HOLINESS: THE LONGING AND THE OBSTACLES

There is a yearning for God in the human heart. It may be unrecognized, and perhaps it can be canceled out by a deliberate choice; but I believe it is still true that, as Saint Augustine said centuries ago, "Our hearts were made for Thee, oh God, and we cannot find rest until we rest in Thee." This, I believe, together with the faithful ministry of the Holy Spirit, is the reason why people sometimes find God even through poor sermons or imperfect witnessing.

God is holy—utterly, absolutely holy, and absolutely morally perfect. As the hymn says,

"Only Thou art holy;
There is none beside Thee
Perfect in power, in love and purity."

More than that, each of us has been created in God's moral likeness. Therefore, I believe, our inner longing for God includes a longing for holiness, a longing to live the kind of life we have known all along we should live—a life of moral and spiritual victory instead of defeat and failure. I am confident that that desire is built into our very nature.

Poets and hymn writers have expressed this longing in beautiful and varied ways:

". . . oh to be like Thee,
Blessed Redeemer, pure as Thou art."
"Would you be whiter, much whiter than snow?
There's power in the blood . . ."

Bible scholars support the concept of a holy life. For example, the late F. F. Bruce, of Plymouth Brethren persuasion, commenting on Phil. 3:10 in the *Good News Commentary*,[1] states that the power of the resurrection of Christ "enables the believer . . . to lead a life of holiness which pleases God." William Hendriksen, a Christian Reformed pastor and scholar, in his comment on the same passage, refers to "this dynamite that destroys sin and makes room for personal holiness . . ."[2] Elisabeth Elliott writes, "God's purpose for us is holiness—his own holiness which we are to share—and the sole route to that end is discipline."[3]

At the same time, on the day-to-day level, a real resistance to personal holiness is all too often encountered—on both theological and personal grounds. Even the hymns about holiness refer much less to *receiving* the grace of holiness than to declaring that it is available or urging the hearer to receive it. Indeed, one gospel song, "Whiter Than Snow," does have a final stanza which reads

> "The blessing by faith I receive from above;
> Oh glory! My soul is made perfect in love.
> My prayer has prevailed, and this moment I know
> The blood is applied; I am whiter than snow."

Unfortunately, most hymnals omit this verse.

Many years ago I heard a godly pastor, Dr. J. M. Knight, of Weekley Memorial United Brethren Church in Charleston, West Virginia, say in a sermon, "If only Christians were as afraid of sin as they are of holiness!" and I fear that that concern is still valid. The fear of holiness may arise in part from a sincere desire not to be hypocritical—not to make a higher claim of piety than the evidence warrants, or not to appear to have a "holier than thou" attitude. Some may have an honest doubt that real personal holiness is possible—the feeling that Romans 7 is the best we can do in this life. At the same time, I suspect that for some Christians

---

[1] *Philippians.* A Good News Commentary, edited by W. Ward Gasque. San Francisco: Harper and Row, 1983, p. 90.

[2] *Philippians.* New Testament Commentary. Grand Rapids: Baker, 1979, p. 168.

[3] *Trusting God in a Twisted World.* Old Tappan, N.J.: Revell, 1989, p. 18.

there is a real fear of what living a holy life would mean, such as giving up some dubious indulgences: "Lord, make me holy—but not yet!"

Beyond these reasons, though, there is a tragic lack of understanding of what biblical holiness really is, even by some who are advocates of holiness. One such misunderstanding is the idea that holiness means "sinless perfection," in which state the person is no longer able to sin. I have personally heard this claim made only by persons outside the holiness circles, such as the barber and part-time preacher who once snorted to my mother, "Humph! These people who think they can get to the place where they can't sin!"—knowing that my parents were among those he was talking about.

If I were confronted now with such a claim, before refuting it I would first like to ask, "Suppose for a moment that God could do something in us that really would make it impossible for us to sin. Would you be a candidate?" In other words, do we really *want* to be free from sin?

Discouragement from a search for holiness is heard on biblical and theological grounds as well. Not long ago I heard Rev. Dennis Appleby, a British evangelist, say that years earlier, when he was a new Christian, in a meeting in which a number of Christian leaders were present he naively asked whether it was possible to be free from sinning in this life. He said that the immediate response from some of those Christian leaders "made it appear as if sin were their best friend!"

The impossibility, or at least the unlikelihood, of holiness in this life is often based on verses of Scripture while other verses that exhort Christians to live a life of holiness are conveniently overlooked. As George Verwer, founder and director of Operation Mobilization, says, "Believers must know the reality of cleansing as we experience the conviction of sin. It is hard to preach holiness and the Lordship of Christ without being accused of perfectionism, but that is our aim—to get our experiences in Christ into practical daily reality."[4]

---

4 "Is the Fire Missing?" in *Decision Magazine*, October 1990, p. 201.

It is sometimes asserted that Romans 7 describes the Apostle Paul's lifelong situation and therefore is the best Christians can hope for in this life. 1 John 1:8 is given as the Christian's state: "If we say that we do not have sin, we deceive ourselves and the truth is not in us," overlooking the promise of the very next verse (1:9): "If we confess our sins, he is faithful and righteous to forgive us our sins and to cleanse us from all unrighteousness." The numerous passages which present holiness as the Christian norm are often dealt with by postulating that these describe a "positional holiness" by which God declares that we are holy even though both God and we know we are not holy in fact.

Some years ago I heard the pastor of a union church across the Pacific say in a sermon, "After we are converted, we continue to live like 'Dirty Sally'"—whoever she was!—"but God looks at Jesus and gives us credit for his sinless life." In another overseas location I heard a graduate of a strong theological seminary tell a Sunday school class that his uncle had been converted as a youth but had turned away from God and lived a very sinful life. "Finally," he said, "the Lord gave up on him and took him home to heaven"! A well-known evangelist in the 1930's declared in his magazine that, when the Lord returns, the roofs of saloons and brothels will blow off as saints rise to meet their Lord!

Fortunately, such extreme statements are the exception; but even the milder form of that point of view I find difficult to reconcile with the many NT passages such as Eph. 1:4, that God has chosen us in Christ "that we should be holy and without blemish before him"; 2 Pet. 3:14, "Therefore, beloved, since you are expecting these things, be diligent to be found by him without spot and without blemish in peace"; Col. 1:22, "God has reconciled you . . . to present you holy and without blemish and irreprovable in his presence."

Even in the Old Testament there are similar passages, such as Ezek. 36:25–26, "I will sprinkle clean water on you, and you will be clean; I will cleanse you from all your impurities and from all your idols. I will give you a new heart and put a new spirit in you . . ." ; and Isa. 35:8–9, "And a highway will be there; it will be called the Way of Holiness. The unclean will not journey on it; it will be for those who walk in that way . . . But only the redeemed will walk there . . ."

In harmony with these passages, there are many, especially followers of John Wesley, who teach and preach that it is God's will for Christians to live a holy life; and there are many people, both laity and clergy, who have testified to a grace of God which enables them to live a holy life—not a life of "sinless perfection," but a life in which spiritual victory is the common level and defeat is the exception.

Chapter 2

THE TWO SIDES OF HOLINESS

At this point, before discussing holiness, it would be well to make clear what we mean by sin. One definition which is sometimes offered is that anything which falls short of the perfect standard of God is sin. With this definition of sin, of course, any talk of deliverance from sin, or victory over sin in this life, is useless. On this definition we all do, as some people say, "sin daily in thought, word, and deed." Such a definition may be useful in reminding us that we should continually seek to improve in our behavior, but I do not find this class of sin to be of great concern in the NT.

The kind of sin with which the NT is concerned, and the kind of sin with which Christians should be concerned, is the kind of sin which we commit knowing that they are sins—"a willful violation of the known will of God." This is the kind of sin from which every Christian should earnestly want to be delivered. This is the spirit of the NT we mentioned in the preceding chapter. If it should be argued that these passages refer only to our condition at the time when we meet God, the implication certainly is *not* that we are free to live otherwise in the meantime!

Let us now look at holiness in the Bible.

Holiness is at the very heart of the religion of the Bible, both in the Old and the New Testaments. Over and over God's holiness is declared, especially in the OT when God was teaching the people about himself. Likewise, the exhortations and commands for God's people to be holy run through both Testaments. J. Baines Atkinson reminds us that holiness is a very practical matter in the OT:

The purpose of the services and sacrifices of the Mosaic tabernacle in the Old Testament was in the first place to make holy men . . . And it is in association with these services we have given the ethical, social and practical obligations of a holy life . . .[5]

He further points out that Lev. 11, following forty-four verses dealing with food, closes with God's command, "Sanctify yourselves therefore, and be ye holy for I am holy," and concludes that food and drink have to do with holiness.[6]

At least eight times in the Pentateuch God commands the people of Israel to be holy (Ex. 22:31; Lv. 11:44–45, 19:2, 6, 20:7, 26; and Num. 15:40); and this exhortation is applied to Christians in 1 Pet. 1:16, "You shall be holy, for I am holy."

Holiness Means to be Set Apart for the Service of a God

The Greek word translated "holy" in the NT is *hagios*. Its basic reference is to anything which is set apart from ordinary use and dedicated to the use or service of a god. In the OT God is described as "holy" over and over; in the prophecy of Isaiah God is referred to as "the Holy One of Israel" some two dozen times. God can be called "holy" in this sense, since as the infinite Being he is utterly separated from all finite created beings.

In this sense of "separation," therefore, any supposed god or religion can have his or its holy persons. Most of us, for example, have heard of Hinduism's "holy men." My earliest knowledge of these holy men was, when I was a child, seeing pictures of Hindu holy men which my father had received from a missionary in India. One picture showed a man who lay all day on a bed of spikes; the other pictured a man who had held his arm pointed upward until it had become rigid and immobile. In recent years, in India I took a picture of a beggar with cow dung plastered in his hair to show that he was a holy man. The "temple women," too, prostitutes associated with Hindu temples, are "holy women." These are indeed holy persons, for they are separated from

5 *The Beauty of Holiness.* London: Epworth Press, 1953, p. 95.

6 p. 97.

ordinary pursuits of life and are dedicated to the service of their gods.

Holiness Means to Share the Characteristics of a God

How, then, do we arrive at the exalted concept of holiness in association with the true God, the God of the Bible? The answer is that, while separation is the basic concept of holiness, there is another concept which is always associated with it. This additional concept is *appropriateness*.

Some people have missed this important aspect of holiness and have understood only the aspect of separation. This point was illustrated humorously by a story which I heard a student pas'or, Valis Hill, give at Roberts Chapel Methodist Church near Harrodsburg, Kentucky, half a century ago. He said that a pastor had been preaching about sanctification as meaning purity of life. One day as he and a farmer parishioner were walking around the farmer's property the farmer commented, "Pastor, I don't agree with your preaching about sanctification. Sanctification is merely separation. Now look at that pig over there. I've separated it from my other pigs to fatten for butchering. So that pig is 'sanctified'; it's separated from the other pigs for me."

"I see," responded the pastor; "and I remember that Hebrews 2:11 says, 'For he who sanctifies and they who are sanctified all have one source; therefore he is not ashamed to call them brothers'!"

This farmer failed to understand that sanctification in its aspect of separation is not the separation of equal things, like a church congregation separated by a middle aisle, or like children dividing jelly beans and saying, "One for me and one for you." The separation of sanctification is rather separation between a lower and a higher level, between things kept for ordinary use and things reserved for the use of a god.

Let me illustrate. When my wife and I do our Christmas shopping (actually, I go with her but she makes the selections), we must look for gifts for adults and for children of various ages. We don't buy crayons and coloring books for our married son, nor do we buy a laptop computer for a newborn baby. The gift needs to be *appropriate* for the recipient. Similarly, a holy object, an object set apart for the use of a god, must be appropriate for that god. A temple prostitute, or a beggar with cow dung in his hair, are appropriate holy persons for gods and a religion characterized by physical and moral filth; a warrior with a blood-stained sword is a proper holy person for a god of war.

Chapter 3

THE CHARACTER OF BIBLICAL HOLINESS

—

What qualities or characteristics, then, are required or appropriate for an object or a person to be "holy" for the God of the Bible? In theological seminary long ago, I learned from John Miley's *Systematic Theology* and Prof. Frank Morris that the three attributes of God are *omniscience, omnipotence,* and *omnipresence*—that is, that he is all-knowing, all-powerful, and everywhere present. However, his principal characteristic, the quality which permeates his attributes and every aspect of his being and activity, is *holiness.* Lest we seem to be defining a word in terms of itself, holiness here means that God is a being of absolute moral perfection and purity. My theology textbook had listed holiness as one of the *predicables,* or qualities, of God, and made the point that holiness was not merely a quality of God but was intensely present in all of his activity. It was soon after studying this topic that I heard the Presbyterian Bible teacher Dr. Harry Rimmer affirm the same idea at the Union Mission Assembly Grounds in Charleston, West Virginia; he declared that holiness is the *absolutely central characteristic* of God. In a similar vein, a book on holiness by Bishop Jesse T. Peck in the last century was entitled *The Central Idea of Christianity.* All of God's other qualities—his love, his justice, his wrath, his mercy—are holy, pure, and perfect.

Indeed, the only morally adequate reason for us to be holy is the fact that God is holy; as he himself says in his Word, "Be holy, *because* I the Lord your God am holy" (italics mine).

It follows, then, that a person or object which is to be holy for God must have qualities which are appropriate for a God of absolute moral perfection and purity. Of course, nothing and no one can fully reflect God's holiness; but holy objects or persons can and must reflect it in some real sense. For example, an animal or object must be free from *physical* defect. In the OT, when God was trying to teach the people of Israel about his holiness, one of the lessons he used was his requirement that animals which were to be sacrificed to him must be free from physical defect—e.g., Ex. 12:5, "year-old males without defect"; Ex. 29:1, "a young bull and two rams without defect"; and many other passages. Indeed, even an Israelite of the priestly class could not officiate as a priest if he had any physical defect, such as if he was "blind or lame, disfigured or deformed; . . . with a crippled foot or hand . . . or has any eye defect . . ." (Lev. 21:16–23).

Why these restrictions? God was not going to eat these animals; even if he did, a bullock with a broken bone, or a sick lamb, would not injure God's health! And could not a priest officiate satisfactorily even if he were a bit disabled? Of course he could; but that was not the point. The point was that these requirements and restrictions were object lessons by which God was teaching his people what he was like; in other words, any person or thing dedicated to God must be without defect, because God was without defect and perfect.

An incident from the life of Mrs. Charles Cowman, whose daily devotional book *Streams in the Desert* is known worldwide, illustrates this principle of appropriateness. She was granted a meeting with Emperor Haile Selassie of Ethiopia, who at that time was in exile in England after Mussolini's forces had occupied his country. Mrs. Cowman decided to present a copy of the New Testament to the emperor, who was a Christian. As I recall the story, Mrs. Cowman bought a deluxe edition of the New Testament, had a velvet-lined box prepared for it, and made a formal presentation of it to the emperor. I am confident that Mrs. Cowman had many times given inexpensive New Testaments or Gospels to people; why take such pains in this case? It was, of course, a matter of appropriateness; the emperor was a person of exalted position, and a gift to him needed to be appropriate for an emperor—it needed to reflect her recognition of *who* he was.

For ordinary persons, however, apart from the restrictions of priests who served God in a special capacity, God's concern was not in the area of physical defect but rather moral and spiritual defect.

God was, indeed, concerned for the health and welfare of his people, and scores of laws and exhortations in the OT were intended to protect their health. These laws were generally set in a religious context, since the people knew very little of the health reasons which would guide or caution us today in these areas. For example, in Lev. 11:24–25 the reason given for prohibiting the eating of certain kinds of sea creatures, birds, and insects is not that they could be the source of harmful germs but that anyone who ate or touched their carcasses would become ceremonially unclean as would anyone touching a person who had certain skin diseases (Lev. 13:3, 8, 15, 20).

However, what was of special concern to God was moral behavior. Sexual immorality of all forms was strictly forbidden (Lev. 18–19). But also forbidden was unethical behavior to others—lying, stealing, defrauding, obstructing justice (Lev. 19:11–14, 33–36), lack of consideration for the poor (Lev. 19:9–10), and a wide spectrum of forms of behavior which were inconsistent with people who belonged to a God of absolute purity and perfection; and, on the other hand, right conduct toward themselves and others was commanded.

In short, in the OT God's holiness and his requirement that his people be holy—morally pure and ethically righteous—affected every aspect of life. In the NT, God is not less concerned for the physical welfare of his people, but the principal emphasis is upon ethical and moral holiness of life. Instead of giving some of the multitude of examples here, however, we will note these as we look in more detail at the various aspects of holiness in the NT.

Is Holiness for Us?

We have pointed out that there is a recognition that Christians ought to be holy, but that there is strong disagreement on whether holiness on some real and recognizable level is possible in this life. What does the NT say on this subject? Does it teach that Christians ought to be holy? More importantly, does it teach that Christians *can* in fact be holy in the full sense of not only being separated for God but also living a life of moral purity, ethical righteousness, and spiritual victory day by day? In order to try to answer these questions, let us turn to the NT itself.

Chapter 4

HOLINESS IN THE NEW TESTAMENT

Since the NT was originally written in Greek, we will have to refer to the Greek text and speak of some Greek words for the basis of our discussion. We will try to be careful not to use Greek words when English words will suffice; however, we will need to make reference to Greek words in order to make some necessary distinctions.

The Vocabulary of New Testament Holiness

The basic Greek word in reference to holiness, as we mentioned previously, is the adjective *hagios*. We call it the basic word because the other words of this family are derived from it. We will discuss the formation of these other words later. As an adjective, *hagios* is translated "holy," as in "Holy Spirit," "holy angels," and "the holy city." In the plural this word is often used as a noun translated "saints," as the Apostle Paul uses it in the introduction to many of his letters to churches and in Eph. 1:4 and Col. 1:22. This word has come into English as a part of such words as *hagiolatry*, which means worship of the saints.

We will have more to say about this word later. However, before moving on it is well to notice that the Latin word for "holy" is *sanctus*. We mention this because a number of words in English dealing with holiness are based on this Latin word; for example, *sanctify*, which means "to make holy," and *sanctification*, which means "the state of being holy" or "the process of becoming holy."

There are several other Greek words related to the basic word *hagios*. We will look at them and their significance a bit later.

Let us now look at holiness in the NT from several points of view.

The Two Aspects of Biblical Holiness

As we indicated earlier, there are two aspects of biblical holiness: separation for the service of God, and moral purity reflecting God's character. The more basic of these two senses is that of separation; however, the aspect of moral purity in the case of holy persons, or the absence of physical defect in the case of animals or objects, is never completely absent.

At the same time, either of these two aspects may be dominant in any given instance, or both may be equally present. For example, the aspect of *separation* for God's service seems to be dominant in passages such as Matt. 4:5, "the holy city"; Matt. 23:17, "the sanctuary that sanctifies the gold"; Luke 2:23, "Every male which opens the womb shall be called holy to the Lord" (quoting Ex. 13:2); John 10:36, "he whom the Father sanctified" (i.e., set him apart for his ministry); and Heb. 9:2, 3, "the holy place," "the holy of holies."

In many other passages, the aspect of *moral purity* is dominant: for example, Eph. 1:4, God "chose us . . . that we should be holy and without blemish before him"; Col. 1:22, "to present you holy and without blemish and irreprovable before him"; Heb. 12:10, "that we might partake of his holiness"; Heb. 12:14, "Pursue . . . holiness, without which no one shall see the Lord"; and 1 Pet. 1:15, "be holy in all your conduct."

In still other passages, both separation and moral purity may be in focus: Mark 6:20, referring to John the Baptist as a "righteous and holy man," separated for God's service and morally pure; and Acts 10:22, "a holy angel."

As we look at holiness from other points of view we will not generally try to point out these two aspects as well, so as not to complicate the discussion. However, these distinctions will be present in each passage and should be considered whenever it is appropriate in order to determine the precise meaning of the passage.

The Levels of Biblical Holiness

We sometimes encounter a feeling, perhaps unconsciously, that a word should have only one level of meaning. The implication is that if we have held to a high level of meaning for a word but then find that it has a lower level of meaning, we must abandon the higher level. This of course is fallacious; many words have more than one level of meaning. For example, if I were to ask my wife for "a drink" she would know that I wanted something no stronger than coffee or a carbonated drink. Some persons, though, in asking for "a drink" would be understood to be asking for something alcoholic. A person who says he "just died from embarrassment" has obviously not died; but that same person may speak of someone else who has "just died" and mean it literally. In past years, a pastor's wife was sometimes respectfully referred to as "the mistress of the parsonage"; but to be called "the mistress of the parson" would have had some very different implications!

Holiness, too, has more than one level of meaning; and it is exceedingly important that we not only recognize that there are these different levels but also understand their significance so as to interpret them correctly in the Bible. Let us now look at holiness from this point of view.

The Holiness of Old Testament Israel

Although we are dealing principally with holiness in the NT, we must include the OT in a discussion of the levels of holiness.

The Israelites of the OT were both exhorted to be a holy people and were called a holy people: Ex. 19:6, "you will be for me a kingdom of priests and a holy nation"; Lev. 11:44–45, "consecrate yourselves and be holy . . . ; therefore be holy" (and similarly 19:2 and 20:7); Deut. 7:6, 14:2, 21, "you are a people holy to the Lord your God"; and Deut. 28:9, "the Lord will establish you as his holy people."

Yet when we read how the people of Israel behaved through their generations, as described in the OT, how could they be called "holy"? The answer, of course, is that, first of all, they were a people whom God had set apart from other nations to serve him. Beyond this, in spite of their failures, sins, and rebellions against

God, their moral life as a nation was distinctly higher than that of their surrounding neighbors.

This is an important point to remember. No matter how far short of God's own character and of his will for them we may think the Israelites were, we must remember that God chose them out of a world that was deeply sinful and degraded, a world of people with little understanding of God and his will and little knowledge of divine resources to enable them to live according to God's will. Indeed, it was because of the sinfulness and degradation of the tribes whom the Israelites encountered as they made their way from Egypt to the Promised Land that God used the Israelites to destroy them. This point is too often overlooked, and the Israelites are sometimes accused of being cruel and bloodthirsty. Even God is condemned; a Methodist bishop some years ago is said to have called the God of the OT "a dirty bully." The second-century heretical teacher Marcion claimed that the OT God was not the same as the God whom Jesus made known.

Yet the OT makes it clear that, in the first place, it was God who was responsible for the destruction of those tribes. In Ex. 34:11 God says, "I will drive out before you the Amorites . . ."; Deut. 7:1 states, "When the Lord your God . . . drives out before you many nations"; and Deut. 7:23 reads, "the Lord our God will drive out those nations before you, little by little."

In the second place, it is clear that it was because of the great sinfulness of those peoples and in order to avoid their sinful influence coming upon the Israelites that God saw that they must be destroyed. This is indicated in passages such as Ex. 34:11–16 and Deut. 7:3–6, 16, which warn the Israelites against making treaties with those peoples or intermarrying with them, "or they will be a snare among you." Moreover, in Josh. 2:8–11 Rahab's plea to the Israelite spies indicates that some of those peoples had heard about the Israelites' God; and she, at least, had believed.

God was dealing with Israel in the light of their circumstances and their understanding. He would doubtless deal with a similar situation today in a different way. But, as my college ethics professor Dr. W. D. Turkington told us in his lectures, "We must judge God not by what we think he should do but by what he is observed to do," since what God does is right.

One level of holiness, then, is the holiness of the nation of Israel in the OT.

The Holiness of All Christians

A higher level than that of the Israelites of the OT is the holiness of every person who has put his faith in Christ for salvation. All Christians, in other words, are "holy" or "saints." Paul addresses some of his letters to the "saints"; these were not a special group noted for exceptional piety, they were all of the Christians. He similarly commends Philemon for his love "for all the saints" (Phlm. 5). In Rom. 1:7 the Apostle refers to his readers as "called saints," meaning "saints by virtue of their call by God," not, as it is commonly understood, "called (by God) to become saints," for they were saints already. In Eph. 3:8 Paul calls himself a saint, even though he humbly claims to be less than the least of them. In many other instances in the epistles he refers to the Christians as "saints." When he says in 1 Cor. 6:11, "but you have been washed, but you have been made holy, but you have been justified," the clear implication is that this holiness took place not later than when they were put right with God through faith in Jesus.

However, in these same letters the Apostle has to deal with sins and failures of these saints, not the least of which was making charges against one another in court, which he mentions in 1 Cor. 6. Nevertheless, these early Christians were holy in a specific sense. By receiving Christ by faith for salvation they were set apart for God. More than this, by their new birth, which resulted in Christ living in them, their lives were on a morally higher level than before, at least inwardly and in many cases outwardly as well.

The same is true of Christians today. In the case of persons who have been saved from lives of wickedness or crime the change is obvious and wonderful. Some of us, then, whose preconversion lives were respectable and upright, from whatever motive, may be inclined to feel that God did not have much of a problem in saving us. But no matter how respectable our lives may have been, no matter how many sins we had not committed, we were not loving God and letting him be our Lord. We were therefore living in violation of what Jesus called "the great and first commandment"; namely, to love God with our whole being (Matt. 22:37–38). So when any of us come to God through Jesus and begin to love and obey God we have made a major move and change of direction. As C. S. Lewis indicated by his characters in *The Great Divorce*, a person who has committed great outward sins may sometimes be nearer to coming to Jesus than even a scholar who delights in theological speculation but who is not interested in finding the real answers in Christ nor submitting himself to God in loving obedience.

Everyone, then, who is a Christian through faith in Jesus is holy, and that holiness is on a higher level than that of the OT Israelites.

A Special Instance: a Lower Level of Holiness

There is one passage in the NT related to holiness which I believe is rarely discussed in reference to this subject. This passage is 1 Cor. 7:12–14. In a later passage, 2 Cor. 6:14, Paul warns Christians against marriage with unbelievers. In the present passage he is dealing with instances in which a believer is already married to an unbeliever. The question might arise as to whether the Christian spouse should separate from the unbelieving partner to avoid being spiritually defiled by such a union. Paul, however, believed that marriage is intended to be permanent. In the present passage he states that, rather than the Christian being defiled by such a marriage, the fact is that the unbelieving spouse is "sanctified," made holy, in some real sense, by union with the Christian spouse. The form of the Greek verb (with which we will deal in more detail later) indicates an event resulting in a present state.

The question is, what level of holiness is this? Does it mean that the unbelieving spouse is born again and has eternal life by being married to a Christian? Of course not. It is true that in most situations we, and I am confident Paul as well, would say that to mix purity with impurity results in impurity. However, the Apostle says that in the case of a mixed marriage, since the two persons have become "one flesh," as Gen. 2:24, Matt. 19:5, and 1 Cor. 6:16 declare, the holiness of the Christian spouse makes the marriage holy and in a limited sense carries over to the unbelieving spouse. On the practical level this would mean that the unbelieving spouse would be to some extent kept from pagan or other evil influences and brought under some degree of Christian influence. However, Paul is probably referring primarily to the unbelieving spouse's participation in the marriage.

Paul reinforces his argument by referring to the children of such a marriage. He says that if what he has said about the marriage is not true, "then your children are spiritually unclean; but in fact they are holy" (v. 14).

In this passage, then, we have a limited sense of holiness, in which the unbelieving spouse and the children are to some extent separated to God and brought under Christian influence, although it certainly does not imply the holiness of a born-again Christian.

A Higher Level of Holiness

Just as there is a level of holiness which is lower than the holiness of every Christian believer, there is also a higher level. In other words, saints—born-again Christians who were made holy when they were regenerated—are called to *become* holy, which clearly implies a different and therefore higher level of holiness.

In 2 Cor. 6:14–18 Paul warns his readers against becoming yoked together with unbelievers; he follows with a collection of OT passages to support his warning. Then in 7:1, turning to the positive aspect, he urges, "Since therefore we have these promises, beloved ones, let us cleanse ourselves from every defilement of flesh and spirit, *completing holiness* in the fear of God." The form of the Greek word translated "completing" implies a process, but the word *complete* itself implies that such a process is to reach completion, with holiness as its result. Here, then, holy persons, as these Corinthians are called in the opening verse of this letter, are exhorted to make the quality of holiness complete in their lives.

In Heb. 3:1 the author refers to his readers as "holy brothers, partakers of a heavenly calling." Then in 12:10 he tells them that God disciplines us for our benefit, "in order that we may partake of his holiness." The form of the verb implies that the "partaking" is to be attained or arrived at, not the continuation of something already achieved. It therefore refers to an attainment subsequent to the new birth; whether it is to occur in this life or at or after death is not overtly indicated and should be decided by a comparison with other passages.

In Heb. 12:14 the author exhorts his readers to "pursue holiness," adding that without holiness "no one will see the Lord." These Christians were already holy and therefore did not need to "pursue" the level of holiness of the new birth. Their pursuit must be for a higher level or development of holiness; and the latter part of the verse implies that the pursuit is intended to enable them actually to grasp the holiness referred to, since without it they could not see the Lord.

In 1 Thes. 3:12–13 the Apostle prays that the Lord will cause them to abound in *agapē* 'love' "in order to *establish your hearts blameless in holiness* before our God and Father at the coming of our Lord Jesus with all his holy ones." It might be argued that this condition is to take place only at the return of Christ; but if they were to be blameless in holiness when Christ returns they must surely become blameless in holiness prior to his coming. However, there is no indication here of any additional event which is to bring about this holiness other than the Lord's work of causing them to abound in love, which surely is intended to take place in their lives at present. Since the verb "to establish" is in the form which implies completion of the action referred to, it is clear that Paul is thinking of their arrival at a state of settled holiness which is beyond the holiness which they received at their new birth.

At the climax of First Thessalonians, Paul returns to the theme of holiness. In 5:23 he prays, "May the God of peace himself make you holy through and through, and may your spirit, soul, and body be kept so as to be blamelessly entire at the coming of our Lord Jesus Christ." Again the form of the verb "to make holy" implies completion of the action, not merely the continuation of something already in progress.

I recently heard a well-known pastor, in a televised message on this passage, saying that this verse describes what is to happen to us when Christ returns. However, if this were Paul's meaning, he surely knew that it was in fact going to happen, and he did not need to pray that it would happen; and his comment would more naturally have been, "And then God will make you completely holy at Christ's return." Further, the preceding verses are exhortations for present and continuing behavior, and the prayer of verse 23 surely fits in logically as something which Paul wanted to take place in the lives of these Thessalonian Christians in their present lives, not merely what he knew would take place at Christ's return.

Verse 24 of this chapter adds the comment, "Faithful is he who calls you, who will also do it." This could be interpreted as words of assurance that God will do this for them when Christ returns, but it seems much more appropriate to see these words as promising that God will do a work in their hearts *now* if they will permit him to do so.

It is clear, then, that *Christians are called to become holy on a higher level than that of conversion.*

Holiness in Heaven

There is surely agreement among Christians that heaven is a holy place, and that everyone who dwells there through the atoning sacrifice of Christ will be fully and perfectly holy. I mention this point only to make it clear that I definitely do not claim that a Christian can attain in this earthly life the perfect holiness of heaven. In this present life we are beset with obstacles to holiness, as the hymn asks: "Is this vile world a friend to grace / To lead me on to God?" Not only outright temptations from Satan and his forces, but also the legitimate cares of our life too easily take our time and occupy our minds and hinder our care for our spiritual welfare. In addition, the limitation of our mind and body hinder us from the full development of mature holiness.

I am not speaking of spiritual defeats and sin; that is another matter. I am saying rather that the things I have just mentioned, and there may be others, tend to limit our development in holiness much as poor soil hinders the growth of a farmer's vegetable garden even though the resulting vegetables might be free of defects.

In heaven, however, the obstacles will be removed, and we will be free to be utterly holy as befits the presence of a God of absolute perfection and purity. Whether we will continue to progress in holiness in heaven, or whether we will immediately be as fully developed in holiness as it is possible for us to be, I do not know. I know only that in this life on earth, after we have been made holy we must grow and mature *in* holiness all our lives—but more about this later.

The Manifestations of Biblical Holiness

We have pointed out that biblical holiness may refer primarily to the aspect of separation to God, or it may refer primarily to the aspect of moral purity for persons or the absence of physical blemish for animals or objects. We have also shown that there is more than one level of holiness. We now want to look at the various ways in which holiness is manifested or represented in the NT. To do this we will examine the various words in the Greek holiness vocabulary; that is, the words which have the same root as the basic word *hagios* 'holy'. In discussing the following words the two aspects of holiness apply, but we will not necessarily mention these areas in order to focus our attention on the point we are emphasizing.

Holiness as a Quality

We referred earlier to the adjective *hagios* 'holy', which is the basic word in the vocabulary of holiness in Greek. We now need to point out that this adjective, like many other adjectives in Greek and in English, describes the *quality* of the noun to which it refers—that is, it tells what *kind* of person or thing it is.

This adjective occurs some 225 times in the NT. Many of these instances refer to the Triune God. For example, some 95 instances refer to the Holy Spirit. Several instances refer to God; for example, John 17:11, "holy Father"; 1 Pet. 1:12, "he who has called you is holy"; 1 Pet. 1:16, "I am holy"; and Rev. 4:8, "Holy, holy, holy, Lord God Almighty." Other instances refer to Jesus, including Luke 1:35, where the angel says to Mary, "that which will be born will be called holy"; John 6:69, "You are the holy one of God"; Acts 3:14, where Jesus is referred to as "the holy and righteous one"; and Acts 4:27, "your holy child Jesus." These three persons of the Trinity are holy, of course; indeed, it is their character that tells us what holiness is.

Angels, too, are called holy; they are set apart for God's service and are morally pure, as is implied in Luke 9:26, Mark 8:38, and Acts 10:22. Their lives are holy in quality.

Many other persons and objects are described as having the quality of holiness. John the Baptist was a "holy man" (Mark 6:20). The prophets were holy (Acts 3:21; 2 Pet. 3:2) and the apostles were holy (Eph. 3:5). The Temple (Matt. 24:15; Acts 6:13), the holy place within the Temple (Heb. 9:2), and the holy of holies (Heb. 9:3) are obviously holy. The OT law is holy (Rom. 7:12), as is the church (Eph. 5:27), the Christian faith (Jude 20), our calling (2 Tim. 1:9), the Mount of Transfiguration (2 Pet. 1:18), and even the kiss of greeting in the church between holy people (1 Cor. 16:20; 2 Cor. 13:12; and 1 Thes. 5:26).

Indeed, we may conclude that everything which is properly Christian is holy, since the very description as "Christian" means that it is in some sense set apart for God and has an appropriate quality.

Most of these instances of the word *holy* simply make statements about the person or object. Some, however, are exhortations or statements of intention or purpose. For example, Eph. 1:4 states that God's purpose for us is that "we should be holy and without blemish before him." Col. 1:22 tells us that Christ's purpose is to present us "holy and without blemish" to God. 1 Pet. 1:15–16 exhorts us that just as God is holy so we should "become holy in all our conduct." Similarly, 2 Pet. 3:11 reminds us that "since all these things are thus going to be destroyed, what sort of persons must you be in all holy manner of life and godliness."

These latter passages make it clear that God's purpose for our lives, and his command, is that we are to be holy. We are God's special people and therefore we are in fact holy in that sense, but we are also to be holy in the sense of reflecting God's moral perfection and purity.

In addition to the adjective *hagios* 'holy', there are two Greek nouns derived from this adjective which likewise express holiness as a quality. These two noun are *hagiōsynē* and *hagiotēs*, both translated 'holiness'. The suffix or final part of each of these

Greek nouns, *-synē* and *-tēs*, indicates quality, just as does the suffix "-ness" in English.

The first of these two nouns, *hagiōsynē*, occurs three times in the NT. In Rom 1:4 Paul tells us that Jesus was "designated Son of God with power by a spirit of holiness" (or possibly "by the Spirit of Holiness," meaning the Holy Spirit). More relevant to our study, however, are the other two instances. In 2 Cor. 7:1 the Apostle urges his readers, "let us cleanse ourselves from every defilement of flesh and spirit, *bringing holiness to completion* in the fear of God." Here the Corinthian Christians, who are "holy people," are urged to make the quality of holiness *complete* in their lives. In 1 Thes. 3:12–13 he prays that the Lord may cause them to abound in love "in order that he may establish your hearts *blameless in holiness*." Here, too, is the clear implication that these holy people need to have the quality of holiness established firmly in their lives.

The second of these nouns, *hagiotēs*, is found in Heb. 12:10, where the author tells his readers that God disciplines us for our benefit, "in order that we may partake of his holiness," the quality of holiness which characterizes God's nature. Its other occurrence is in 2 Cor. 1:12, where Paul's boast is that "by the grace of God" he has lived "in holiness and sincerity" in the world.[7]

We see, then, that both by the adjective "holy" and by the two nouns translated "holiness" the NT not only describes Christians as holy but also *exhorts them to be completely holy.*

Holiness as a State or Condition

One of the forms or tenses of Greek verbs is called the "perfect" tense. Years ago, before I was married, I was attempting to help the students in my Greek class, some of whom were married, to understand the meaning of this tense. "The Greek perfect tense," I said, "describes a *state* resulting from a *previous*

---

[7] We should point out that instead of "holiness" a number of Greek manuscripts have a word meaning "sincerity," which would result in two words with very similar meanings in this verse, as the KJV has it, "simplicity and sincerity." However, "holiness" is much better supported in the Greek manuscripts, and both the RSV and the NIV read "holiness" here.

action. For example, it is like marriage. A married person is in a state resulting from the previous event of the marriage ceremony."

At this, one of my married students piped up, "Yes, Professor, marriage really is the perfect state!"

The illustration fits well. There is a different form of the verb, called the "aorist" tense, which refers simply to a past event; the perfect tense, however, refers to a present state which has resulted from that past event. In that sense, to say "I am forgiven" using the perfect tense means "God forgave me, and I am now forgiven."

It is not always easy to express this concept in English without adding words of explanation. For example, "I have eaten" may mean merely "I have finished my meal"; but this same statement in the afternoon of Thanksgiving Day may reflect the Greek perfect tense and mean "I ate a big dinner and am still feeling the effects!"

This form of the verb is very meaningful. For example, in 1 John 1:1 the writer states that he is declaring "what we *have heard*, what we *have seen* with our eyes." Both of these verbs are in the perfect tense and mean that John not only saw and heard Jesus years ago but that that experience still affects his life—he is in a condition resulting from having seen and heard Jesus. In 2 Tim. 1:12 Paul says, "I know him whom I *have believed*"; he was now in a condition resulting from having put his faith in Jesus. 1 Cor. 1:23, 2:2, and Gal. 3:1 refer to "Christ crucified"—no longer on the cross but forever carrying the redeeming results of that crucifixion.

It will not be surprising to know, then, that the perfect tense of the Greek verb *hagiazō* 'to make holy' is significant, meaning to be in a state resulting from having become holy. This verb occurs 27 times in the NT, including eight instances in the perfect tense. Let us now look at some of these eight passages.

In John 17:19, Jesus in his prayer to the Father says, "for their sake I sanctify myself in order that they themselves may be in a sanctified condition"; that is, that they may be in a condition resulting from having been made holy.

In Acts 20:32 Paul tells the elders of the Ephesian church that God is able to give them "the inheritance among all the sanctified ones," those who were in a state resulting from having been made holy. Acts 26:18 similarly refers to an inheritance "among the sanctified ones," and 1 Cor. 1:2 calls the Christians "sanctified ones," believers who have been made holy in the past and are now in that condition. In 2 Tim. 2:21 Paul tells Timothy that if anyone will cleanse himself from unworthy things he will be "sanctified, fit for the Master"; that is, in a condition resulting from having been made holy. Heb. 10:10 states that "by God's will we are sanctified"—that is, in a condition resulting from having been made holy.

Holiness as a state is also expressed by a noun, *hagiasmos* 'holiness'. You will notice that we gave "holiness" as a translation of the Greek noun expressing holiness as a quality; here, however, the meaning is holiness as a state, which is indicated by the suffix *-mos*. The two concepts of holiness as a state and as a quality are somewhat similar, but for our purposes it is important to keep them separate. The word *sanctification*, too, is sometimes used in another sense, but here it refers to holiness as a state.

This noun occurs ten times in the NT. Rom. 6:19 exhorts the readers to present the members of their bodies to God "as servants for righteousness for the purpose of a state of holiness." Similarly, in Rom. 6:22 the Apostle says, "having been freed from sin and having become enslaved to God, you have holiness as ycur fruit"; that is, the result of this relationship to God is a state of holiness or sanctification.

1 Thes. 4:2–3 states that the will of God for these Christians is "your sanctification," meaning that they should be in a state of holiness. One purpose of this state of holiness, the Apostle goes on to say, is that they may abstain from sexual immorality. Verse 3 states the further purpose that they may each "possess his own vessel in a state of holiness." Whatever the word "vessel" may mean here, and the interpretations are legion, it is intended to be done in a state of holiness or sanctification.

Heb. 12:14 urges the readers to "pursue peace (as a state) and the state of holiness, apart from which no one shall see the Lord." The Greek text makes it clear that the two Greek words translated "apart from which" mean "apart from the state of holiness," not "apart from peace" nor "apart from peace and holiness."

1 Cor. 1:30 states that Christ "has become wisdom to us from God, namely justification and the state of holiness and redemption."

Christians, then, are called to live in a state of holiness.

To summarize, we have spoken of holiness as a description or *quality* of a person or object, and holiness as a *state* or condition of life. Holiness as a quality may be inherent—that is, it may have existed from the beginning—or it may have been acquired at a later time. This may be true also of holiness as a state when it is expressed by either of the two nouns we have just referred to. On the other hand, when the state or condition of holiness is expressed by the perfect tense of the verb, the implication, as we stated above, is that it is not an inherent condition but rather a condition that has resulted from a preceding event.

Holiness as an Event

Let us now look at the *event*, or events, which produce holiness.

We stated above that the noun *hagiasmos* indicates holiness as a state in some passages. In addition, this noun refers to holiness as an action or event in two passages which are very similar in their meaning. 2 Thes. 2:13 states that the readers have been chosen for salvation "by sanctification of the Spirit"; and 1 Pet. 1:2 addresses the readers as "chosen sojourners . . . by sanctification of the Spirit." The reference in both of these passages seems clearly to be to an *action* by the Holy Spirit to make these Christians holy.[8] The much more common manner of describing holiness as an event or occurrence, however, is by the aorist tense of the Greek verb, which we mentioned earlier. This tense has two principal uses. It refers to an action which has occurred in the past. In addition, in commands and some other types of expression it refers to an action as completed without

---

[8] An alternative interpretation, "by sanctification of your spirit," is less likely, but it would equally refer to an action or event to make them holy.

stating when it occurred or will occur. Our English language furnishes abundant examples of this concept: "He built a house," "I want to buy a car," "I saw him fall," "Shut the door," "You should eat your lunch." The verbs in all of these examples focus on the *completion* of the action without indicating how long a time was required.

This Greek tense is the natural tense to use to refer to an event or action which is instantaneous, but instantaneousness is not its principal sense. For example, this tense would be used in a sentence like "Build me a house," although building a house is not accomplished in an instant. The principal emphasis of this tense is completion. To look at it slightly differently, this tense looks at an action as a single completed event, in contrast with an action which continues or is repeated over and over.

This form of the verb is used, for example, in John 11:39, where Jesus at the tomb of Lazarus commands, "Take away the stone!" and in verse 41, "They took away the stone." It is found in Acts 16:31, where Paul says to the Philippian jailer, "Believe on the Lord Jesus," meaning "Put your faith in Jesus" (as a completed act). It occurs in Rom 5:1, "having been justified by faith" (as a completed fact).

With this introduction, let us examine the usage of the verb *hagiazō* 'to make holy' as it is used in this sense of a completed action in the NT.

Matt. 23:17 refers to "the sanctuary which sanctifies the gold" as a completed fact.

In John 10:36 Jesus refers to himself as the one "whom the Father sanctified." Of course, Jesus did not need to be sanctified in the sense of being made morally pure; the sense here is that the Father sanctified him by setting him apart (as a completed fact) for his earthly ministry.

Two passages refer to our actions toward God and toward Jesus. In the Lord's Prayer (Matt. 6:9 and Luke 11:2) we read, according to the KJV, "Hallowed be thy name"—that is, "May your name be kept holy." 1 Pet. 3:15 exhorts us, "Sanctify Christ as Lord in your hearts." But how can we human beings make God's name holy, or make Christ holy in our hearts? The answer is well given by a commentator from an earlier day, quoted in Alford's commentary on this verse: "Care only for this, that your heart may be a temple of Christ, in which becoming honour may be given to Him as Lord."[9]

In 1 Cor. 6:11 Paul writes, "you were washed, you were sanctified, you were justified." Each of these three verbs refer to a completed action, describing three aspects of their conversion. The sanctification, therefore, is doubtless the holiness received in the new birth.

Eph. 5:25–27 states that "Christ loved the church and gave himself for it in order that he might sanctify it, cleansing it by the washing of the water in the word, in order to present the church to himself as a glorious thing, not having spot or wrinkle or any such thing, but that it might be holy and without blemish." Here both aspects of holiness, set apart for himself and made morally and spiritually pure, are in focus. The verb "sanctify" implies a completed act, and so do the words "cleansing" and "present." The context does not specify a definite time when these actions take place, whether at conversion, some subsequent time, or at the Resurrection. The important point in this passage is that Christ's intention is for his people to be holy, and the implication is that it is Christ who makes them holy.

Heb. 13:12 states that Jesus suffered "in order that he might sanctify the people through his own blood." The context does not indicate when this sanctification was to occur, but the point is that Christ's death was, in fact, intended to make his people holy.

In 1 Thes. 5:23 Paul prays, "May the God of peace himself make you completely holy, and may your spirit, soul, and body be kept so as to be blameless and entire at the coming of our Lord Jesus Christ." We referred to this passage earlier as a clear example of a level of holiness above the holiness of the new birth, for not only were these Thessalonians already Christians, and therefore holy, but Paul also spoke highly of their lives and conduct. Yet in this verse he uses the verb form of completed action in his prayer that God would "make them holy," and he

---

[9] Henry Alford, *The Greek Testament*, Vol. 4, Part 1. London: Rivingtons, 1859, p. 362.

adds to the verb a word which means "in every part" or "completely." Clearly, then, the holiness Paul prays for in this passage is on a higher level than the holiness of the new birth, and he prays that God would grant it as an event later than the new birth. The Greek verb translated "kept" implies that this holiness will have been obtained earlier than the time of Christ's return.

Heb. 10:29 refers to a person who has rejected Christ and has considered the blood of the covenant, "by which he was sanctified, as an unclean thing." When he was sanctified is not indicated; it could have been at his conversion. But it is clear that at some point he was indeed made holy, or sanctified.

Christians, then, are called to become holy.

Holiness, or sanctification, then, is not only a *quality* of the Christian life and the *state* or condition in which Christians are to live, but it is also an *event* which is to take place in our lives—at conversion on one level, but also on a deeper level in which our lives are made holy "in every portion." The significance must not be missed: the instances we have quoted in this section do not refer to the beginning of a process from uncleanness to holiness, nor to the continuation of such a process, but rather to an action or event which is to take place and be completed. In some of the passages it is not clear when this event is to occur; in others it refers to a sanctification at conversion; but in other passages, such as 1 Thes. 5:23, it is clearly an event subsequent to conversion.

Holiness as a Process

Holiness is a process; doubtless almost every serious Bible student would agree with that proposition. I have heard it said that "conversion is an event; holiness is a lifelong process." Some, indeed, have claimed that the followers of John Wesley believe that by one "second work of grace" they are transported to a level of holiness beyond which there is no need to advance; they have become as holy as it is possible to be in this life. A number of years ago I heard the late Dr. M. R. DeHaan, in one of his messages on the well-known "Radio Bible Class" broadcast, put forth this view. I wrote to him, telling him that he had misunderstood the Wesleyan viewpoint, and I set forth briefly what I believe was in fact the Wesleyan position. I received a very gracious response from Dr. DeHaan, in which he thanked me for my letter and commented, "I heartily agree with you in your letter that our points of view on this vital matter are not nearly as far apart as we might imagine."[10]

We must therefore point out an important distinction between two very different senses of holiness as a process. It is one thing to refer to progress *in* holiness, in which a person who has become holy on some level continues to become more and more holy. Quite a different matter is the concept of a process *into* holiness, by which a person little by little moves from unholiness to holiness. Unfortunately, these two very different senses are too often not properly distinguished, and the result is confusion and misunderstanding.

What about the Process of Becoming Holy?

Since we have looked at holiness as an event which occurs and becomes complete in a specific sense, especially as indicated by the aorist verb tense, let us look for passages which refer to holiness as a process of *becoming* holy.

Just as there is one Greek verb tense, the aorist, which indicates an action as completed, and another, the perfect tense, which refers to a state or condition resulting from an event, so there is a tense which indicates a process or continuation; this is the present tense. Parenthetically, it is worth noting that this tense is used in every instance in the NT which states that believing gives eternal life, as in John 3:16 and 20:31. In other words, in the NT eternal life is based on *continuing* to believe, not merely on one act of belief.

We must notice, however, that this continuation may be in one of two forms. On the one hand, it may describe the continuation of one action or state, as in John 1:32, "I beheld the Spirit *coming down* as a dove from heaven," in which John the Baptist indicates that he observed the progress of the dove's flight downward. On the other hand, the process may consist of the repetition of an action even though each action is completed. For example, this form of the verb is found in John 1:33, where John

---

[10] Personal letter, October 29, 1954.

the Baptist says that God sent him "to baptize in water," meaning that he was to perform many baptisms, not one continuing baptism of one person. Similarly, in Acts 2:47, "those who were being saved daily" were a series of persons, each of whom became saved in a completed sense.

Let us now look for examples in which the verb *hagiazō* refers to a process. Of the twenty-eight occurrences of this verb in the NT, twelve are in the aorist tense, referring to a past event, nine are in the perfect tense, indicating a condition resulting from a previous event, and three are in forms which are not relevant to our discussion. This leaves four examples of the present tense, indicating a continuation or process, two of which are in the same verse.

Matt. 23:19 refers to "the altar which sanctifies the gift"— that is, "the altar which makes the gift holy." Grammatically, this could mean that the altar gradually makes the gift holy, but this is a very unlikely interpretation for this situation; there is no reason why the altar would not make the gift holy at the moment when the gift is laid on it. Just two verses earlier, Matt. 23:17, reads, "the sanctuary which sanctifies the gold," in which the verb "sanctifies" is in the aorist tense, referring to a completed act. Matt. 23:19, then, clearly refers to the sanctifying of a continuing stream of gifts placed upon it, each gift being sanctified as a completed act.

Heb. 2:11 includes the present tense of this verb twice. Referring to what Jesus does for his people, this verse reads, "For he [i.e., Jesus] who sanctifies and they [i.e., his people] who are being sanctified all have one origin." The same form is found in Heb. 10:14, "For by one offering he [i.e., Jesus] has perfected forever those who are being sanctified." Grammatically, these two passages could mean that Jesus gradually makes people holy and that his people are gradually being made holy. Equally valid grammatically, however, is the interpretation of Heb. 2:11 that Jesus makes each person holy as a definite and completed act, and that the people referred to in Heb. 2:11 and 10:14 are individually made holy as a completed act. The process or continuation is the progression of people who come to Jesus to be made holy, as is the case of the gifts on the altar in Matt. 23:19. It is significant that these are the only NT examples of this verb which indicate a process.

Which of these two interpretations we have just given, then, is most likely the author's meaning in these two verses? Notice that each of these four instances of the verb, while they can grammatically be interpreted to mean a process of becoming holy, can at least equally well (and Matt. 23:19 almost certainly) refer to a procession of completed acts. This means that *there are no instances at all in the NT in which the verb* hagiazō *'to make holy' clearly refers to sanctification as a process or gradual development from unholiness to holiness.* On the other hand, as we have pointed out earlier, there are twelve instances in which sanctification or becoming holy is clearly referred to as an act which is completed, and nine additional instances in which sanctification is referred to as a state resulting from a previous act.

There are two other passages which we should perhaps include in this discussion, even though the verb "to make holy" does not occur in them. One of these is 2 Cor. 7:1, "let us cleanse ourselves from every defilement of flesh and spirit, completing holiness in the fear of God." "Holiness" in this verse is the noun which means "the quality of holiness." The word "completing" is in the present tense, which refers to a process or continuation; so one interpretation of this verse could be a reference to moving from unholiness to holiness. However, the verb "let us cleanse" in this verse is in the aorist tense, which indicates that the cleansing is intended to be completed. Moreover, even though the form of the word "completing" indicates a process, the very meaning of the word itself, as we stated earlier, indicates that this process is intended to become finished and completed.

The other passage is Heb. 12:14, "Pursue peace with all people, and holiness, apart from which no one shall see the Lord." First, as we mentioned some time back, the word "which" is singular in Greek, and the form (the grammatical gender) of this word shows that it refers only to "holiness," not to "peace" nor to both nouns. The verb "pursue" is in the present tense, indicating a process or continuation, and of course the very meaning of the verb suggests a process. However, the writer of this valuable letter is urging not merely the *pursuit* of holiness; he means that his readers should *obtain* the state of holiness, since he warns that "apart from" this state of holiness "no one shall see the Lord." What the writer is saying here, in other words, is, "Be continually pursuing peace with all people, and be continually pursuing the state of holiness; without this state of holiness no one shall see the Lord."

Holiness, then, according to the NT, is referred to as an act or *event* which is to take place in our lives; it is a *state* or condition resulting from a prior event; and it is a *quality* which is to characterize our lives. The one passage which most nearly seems to indicate a *process* of becoming holy (2 Cor. 7:1) also clearly implies that that process is to be completed.

If what we have said is true—and I do not see how it can be proved otherwise—then it appears that a good deal of preaching and teaching about holiness has been mistaken. *Holiness is intended to take place in our lives, producing a state and a quality in us that enables us to say,* joyfully but in deep humility and gratitude, recognizing that it is nothing we have done but rather is God's gracious gift, *"God in his grace has made me holy!"* Surely such a testimony is no more "presumptuous" than a testimony that "God in his grace has saved me." On the other hand, *there is no clear NT teaching that moving from unholiness to holiness is a gradual process.*

The Process of Increasing in Holiness

Although we are insisting that holiness is a state which can be arrived at, we want to make it clear that we do not consider such an event as "the end of the line," as a state in which no further spiritual development is necessary or possible. Quite the opposite is true. If a farmer succeeds in clearing the weeds from his garden completely, this does not mean that his crops are automatically and immediately mature; on the contrary, the weeds are cleared so as to enable the crops to grow and develop. Similarly, when God by his work of sanctification cleanses the weeds of unclean words, habits, and thoughts from our lives, it makes possible the spiritual growth and development **in** holiness which is the Christian norm.

Ruth Graham, in her book, *Legacy of a Packrat*,[11] quotes the renowned pianist Arthur Schnabel as saying that "great music" is "music composed better than it can be played." Yet it can be, and often is, played well, and doubtless well enough to have satisfied the composer. Similarly, holiness in its utter perfection is higher than we can attain in this life. Yet by God's grace we can be holy in a real sense with which God is pleased, not merely a positional fiction.

For NT references to this growth, however, we will have to look outside the uses of the verb we have been discussing, for the verb *hagiazō* means 'to sanctify', 'to make holy', not 'to be holy'.[12] Growth in holiness is presented, rather, in more general terms. Here are some examples:

- Col. 1:10 speaks of "growing in the true knowledge of God"; Col. 2:7 refers to "being (more and more) rooted and grounded in him (Christ) and being (more and more) confirmed in the faith"; and Col. 2:19 states that from Christ as head "all the body ... grows the growth that God intended."
- 2 Pet. 3:18 urges, "be growing in grace and knowledge of our Lord and Savior Jesus Christ." In 1 Thes. 4:1 Paul urges his readers, "just as you have received from us how it is necessary for you to walk and to please God, just as you are even walking, that you would abound more"; and in 4:10, speaking of brotherly love, he recognizes that they are doing this but urges them "to abound more."
- Eph. 3:19 speaks of "becoming filled up into all the fullness of God"—that is, coming into full Christian maturity. Eph. 4:12-16 refers to "building up the body of Christ, until we all arrive at the unity of the faith and the true knowledge of the Son of God, into mature manhood, into the measure of the stature of the fullness of Christ," and the harmonious working of every part of the body of Christ, causing it to "build itself up in love." Eph. 5:8-10

---

11 Nashville: Thomas Nelson, 1989, p. 204.

12 The lone exception is Rev. 22:11, "and let him who is holy *be holy* still," but the Greek of Revelation is irregular.

urges, "Be walking as children of light ... examining what is well-pleasing to the Lord."

- In Phil. 1:9-11 Paul prays "that your love may still abound more and more in true knowledge and all perception, so that you may test the things that differ, in order that you may be sincere and without offense for the day of Christ, filled with the fruit of righteousness which is through Jesus Christ for the glory and praise of God."

Of course, much of the NT epistles deal with exhortations or instructions on developing our spiritual life. There is no apparent effort by the authors to distinguish between progress in the Christian life in one level of holiness or another. The assumption is that Christians are to live pure and holy lives, that if they are not holy in this sense they are to permit God to make them so, and that during all their lives they are to grow and develop in holiness and love.

Holiness—When?

We have shown that holiness is indicated in the NT as an event, something which is intended to happen, to take place in our lives. We have also shown that holiness exists at more than one level. Let us now examine more specifically the question of *when* holiness is intended to take place, although we have dealt with this point, in part, earlier.

In some passages it is not specified when the sanctification is to take place, whether at the new birth or subsequently. The point being made in these passages is simply the fact that the believer is to be made holy. These passages include 2 Thes. 2:13, "God has chosen you as firstfruits for salvation through sanctification by the Spirit"; 1 Pet. 1:1-2, "chosen sojourners ... through sanctification by the Spirit"; Heb. 10:29, referring to a person who "has considered the blood of the covenant, by which he was sanctified, an unclean thing"; and Heb. 13:12, which states that Jesus suffered outside the camp "in order that he might sanctify the people through his own blood."

In 1 Cor. 6:11, the sequence "washed ... sanctified ... justified" implies that all three of these actions occurred at the new birth.

Now, however, let us look at some other passages:

- Eph. 5:25-27 tells us that Christ gave himself for the Church "in order that he might make her holy ... in order that he might present the church to himself as a glorious thing, not having spot or wrinkle or any of such things, but that she might be holy and without blemish." This passage certainly speaks of making the church holy on a level of holiness which is above the holiness of the new birth, and must therefore be an event which takes place subsequent to regeneration.
- 1 Thes. 5:23 clearly refers to a level of holiness above the holiness of the new birth; the Apostle's prayer for these "holy people" is, "May the God of peace himself make you completely holy" so that they will be "blameless and entire at the coming of our Lord Jesus Christ."
- Heb. 12:14 urges Christian believers, who are already holy people, to "pursue holiness," which would necessarily be a higher level of holiness, and implies that this holiness or sanctification is a realizable goal since without it "no one shall see the Lord."
- 2 Cor. 7:1 urges these believers to "bring holiness to completion," which is clearly a higher level than they had already attained.

We conclude, then, that we are sanctified, made holy, when we are born again. But we further conclude that *there is a deeper level of holiness which believers are urged to receive, as a definite event, in this life.*

Chapter 5

HOLINESS: OUR RESPONSIBILITY

If what we have said is true, then what should we do? What we should do, both as our privilege and as our obligation, is to receive this gift of cleansing and victory which God has provided for us. In doing so, we will join a great host, from past ages and from the present, from many lands and languages, who have lived this life of holiness.

Nor is this life the privilege of only one theological group. It is true that John Wesley is the one who brought this teaching to prominence, yet many people whose theology differed at some points from Wesley have entered into this experience as well. Henry Clay Morrison, in the Wesleyan tradition, was one of the great holiness evangelists of the late nineteenth and much of the twentieth centuries. Yet, as Ken Abraham relates in his book, *Positive Holiness*,[13] when Morrison was a young pastor, clearly born again but deeply aware of the inconsistencies and internal conflict in his life, it was a godly Presbyterian pastor who directed him into this victory which radically changed the rest of Morrison's life and preaching. "We Presbyterians call this 'the life of faith,' the pastor told him, "but John Wesley, your patron, called it 'Perfect Love,' or 'Entire Sanctification.'"

E. Stanley Jones, the noted Methodist missionary to India, tells how it was through reading Hannah Whitall Smith's *The Christian's Secret of a Happy Life* that he was led into this experience which cleansed and consecrated every aspect of his life to Christ.[14]

---

13 Old Tappan, N.J.: Revell, 1988, pp. 93–94.

14 From *A Song of Ascents*, quoted in *Positive Holiness*, pp. 172–75.

Abraham goes on to tell how F. B. Meyer, at one time president of the World Baptist Alliance, after a struggle in which, he says, "I thought I would die," was able to surrender his life completely to God and received the cleansing and filling. As a result his ministry became profoundly effective, and his books are still bringing blessing to many people.[15]

He describes the experience of Norman Vincent Peale, long-time pastor of New York's Marble Collegiate Church (of the Reformed Church), who at a time of tension and self-doubt cried out to Jesus, "Fill me with your Holy Spirit," and received a cleansing and peace which remained with him, "the greatest experience of my life."[16]

He tells how John Wesley White, for many years an associate evangelist with the Billy Graham ministries, in 1987 at a meeting in Rochester, New York, having come to realize his need of holiness, proceeded to acknowledge his need to his audience, then preached a sermon on holiness. At the close of the sermon he went to the altar himself with many others to pray for and receive heart cleansing and holiness.[17]

I am confident that many Christians have entered the life of holiness, calling the experience by other names and perhaps by no name, and possibly without even recognizing it as an event at the time but only aware of the resulting victory in everyday life. In the final analysis, the crucial question is, "Is my heart clean and my life holy now?"

Let me say once again that holiness received is necessarily a mandate for growth and maturity in holiness. I confidently affirm, however, and I believe our study of the Greek NT makes it clear, that the move from the partial holiness of the new birth to the deeper level of full holiness or entire sanctification is *not* intended to be a gradual process, but an event.

A few years ago I gave a lecture on holiness based on the Greek text of the NT to a group of students in a school associated with a Wesleyan ministry. Following the lecture I gave the

---

[15] Pp. 178–80.

[16] Pp. 96–98, quoting Peale's book, *The Positive Power of Jesus Christ.*

[17] Pp. 102–05.

opportunity for questions from the audience. I was caught off guard when a Christian leader who was present very pointedly asked me, "What if I believe that holiness comes as a process?"

As I recall, since I didn't want to have a confrontation with the questioner I gave some mild reply. Perhaps I should have equaled his frankness with a story I heard Dr. Henry Clay Morrison tell. Dr. Morrison was an eloquent preacher, and he was often invited to preach for pastors who did not fully agree with his doctrine of holiness.

On one occasion, as Dr. Morrison told the story, a pastor for whom he was preaching said to him, "Dr. Morrison, you and I are not very far apart. We both believe in holiness; you believe it comes as a definite experience, and I believe it comes as a gradual process."

"Well," Dr. Morrison replied, "do you know of anyone who has come into holiness as a gradual process?"

"No, I guess not," the pastor responded.

"Then it looks like I preach it like it happens, and you preach it like it doesn't!"

Hannah Whitall Smith tells a similar story, in *Christian's Secret*.[18] In one of her meetings a lady asserted that she believed in growing into holiness. Asked how long she had been growing, "About twenty-five years," she replied. "And how much more unworldly and devoted to the Lord are you now than when your Christian life began?" inquired Mrs. Smith. "Alas!" she replied. "I fear I am not nearly so much so!"

Even so, if someone can testify that he has entered into holiness by a gradual process, I will rejoice with him; for—let me say it again—my principal concern is not with the doctrines, the terms, nor the methods, but rather "Am I holy now?"

Nor will I object if someone can testify that God cleansed his heart and brought him into a state of holiness when he was converted. A one-time colleague of mine once said to me, "We

---

18 Chapter 14.

get it all at conversion, and if we need anything afterward it is because we lost something we had."

I won't declare that what my colleague said never happens. I am confident, however, that common experience and the NT message is that at conversion we receive peace and a sense of forgiveness that fills us with joy. Then later the Holy Spirit begins to show us that there is something remaining in our hearts that needs to be dealt with to make us truly holy, not that we have lost something we had received.

We can, of course, refuse this grace. Many Christians, I fear, believe that the best we can do in this life too nearly resembles the defeated life described in Romans 7. But God has something better for us in this life; and it is by not realizing the possibility of this grace, or by refusing to accept it, that the situation of Rom. 7:25 results, in which, depending solely on our own resources without the grace of God, as the text implies, our lives will be lives of conflict and defeat.

What Does Holiness Do?

In discussing the effect of holiness in a Christian's life, perhaps we should first point out what it does not do. It does not change our personality type, making an extrovert out of an introvert. It does not remove physical or mental handicaps. It does not prevent us from making mistakes nor from being tempted. However, by being freed from much of the baggage of inner conflict we can give expression to our personality in more gracious ways.

Moreover, neither holiness nor its opposite, carnality, can be measured in decibels; that is, neither loudness nor silence in themselves indicate either holiness or carnality. "Hallelujah! Praise the Lord!" shouted with one or both arms raised may reflect deep spiritual commitment or superficial extroversion; and the person who sits quietly may be rejoicing in the Lord inwardly or may have no spiritual joy to express.

Let me illustrate this point. I remember two college students, both of whom were vocal and emotional in their testimonies. One of these students then went to a theological seminary known for its unbelief, and I was told that within a year this student was just as vocal in his worldliness. The other student, Bob Barefoot, went to his home state to preach. I heard that his denominational superintendent urged him not to preach holiness, but Bob insisted that he must preach it. A few short years later, a truck loaded with hot tar coming down a mountain road struck Bob's car, burning and injuring him mortally. But before he died in the hospital he was able to rejoice that he had been faithful to the message and life of holiness.

On the other hand, quietness may indicate a holy peace or it may cover deep resentment and hostility. We all doubtless know persons who when they are crossed or offended do not respond with an angry outburst; but even though they may say or do little we know to walk softly and stay out of their way for a while. Then there are those who may never shout "Hallelujah!" but whose quiet demeanor clearly reflects the deep peace of God and the joy of the Lord.

Somewhere, long ago, I read of two Quaker ladies who were walking along the street when a young man dashed by them and carelessly but not intentionally splashed muddy water from a puddle onto the dress of one of the women. The young man immediately stopped and apologized, and the lady accepted his apology. As the youth went on his way, her companion commented on how sweetly she had responded to the young man. "Aye," the other replied, "but thee did not see the boiling inside!"

On the other hand, silence or a quiet response to an unpleasant circumstance may be, and I am confident can be, an indication of peace and the absence of resentment by the power of the Holy Spirit. This is holiness in action.

What, then, does holiness do for the Christian in a practical everyday way?

The heart of the matter is the heart! In other words, holiness of heart purifies the motives behind our thoughts, words, and actions. When I rebuke, spank, or otherwise discipline my small child, I may do the identical disciplining either with resentment in my heart against the child or with inner peace and hurting that my child has misbehaved. When someone else is chosen to sing the solo in the choir, I may carnally resent that my superior talent was ignored or I may with a pure heart be glad for the other person's opportunity to sing. When someone else wins over me in the election to public office, I may hold my resentment against my opponent and the unintelligent public who voted for him, or I may be at peace in the conviction that I did my best even if I am troubled about my opponent's policies.

Pride, ambition, even anger—these and other attitudes and emotions are neither good nor evil in themselves. Pride that makes me want to take proper care of myself and do my best is good and is consistent with holiness; pride that makes me arrogant and egotistical is carnal. I ought to have a holy, God-inspired anger against abuse of children or adults and against political or moral corruption. But when anger produces a carnal spirit in my heart that causes me to hate a person, it is sinful.

I suppose one of the areas of holiness which is prominent in my own thinking is the area of victory over carnal anger. Perhaps this is in part because my earliest childhood memory of hearing about holiness is hearing my mother say that in her youth she had temper outbursts, but "when the Lord sanctified me, he freed me from my temper"; and I saw that testimony supported by her life for forty years until her death.

I suppose we all have heard someone say, "Oh, I know I have a temper, and I really get mad; but I get over it quickly." I want to respond, "Yes, but how quickly do the victims of your anger recover? A bomb blast gets finished quickly, too; but the damage it causes can be terribly lasting!"

Ruth Tucker, in her book *Sacred Stories*,[19] tells that the great evangelist Dwight L. Moody struggled with his temper. On one occasion, as a meeting was about to begin, a man came up to Moody and deliberately insulted him. Moody reacted violently, pushing the man down a stairway. A few minutes later, as he opened the meeting, the evangelist publicly acknowledged his wrong to the audience and asked forgiveness of the man he had pushed.

Jeffrey R. Holland, a former president of Brigham Young University, is quoted in *Reader's Digest*[20] as saying, "One lament

---

19 Grand Rapids: Zondervan, 1989, p. 201.

20 "Points to Ponder," Oct. 1990, p. 131.

I cannot abide is the poor, pitiful, withered cry, 'Well, that's just the way I am.' Spare me your speeches. I've heard them from too many people who wanted to sin and call it psychology."

What about Failure?

Entering into the experience and life of holiness is no guarantee of lifetime perfect performance nor automatic insurance against failure. The Christian life, both in the new birth and in the life of holiness, is a life of faith. God's grace, the power of the Holy Spirit, and the indwelling Christ, can give us moment-by-moment victory. Can you think of any sin that God's power could not keep us from committing? Neither can I.

If I as a Christian commit a sin, it seems to me that there are three possibilities: 1) God could have kept me from sinning, but he didn't care enough to do so; 2) God wanted to keep me from sinning, but he wasn't powerful enough to do so; or 3) God wanted to keep me from sinning, and he could have done so, but I failed to let him. The correct alternative is obvious, isn't it?

We can grow careless for any number of reasons and in a moment of weakness fail to let God keep us victorious; as a result, we can fall victim to temptation and sin. One verse of the hymn, "Come Thou Fount," reads

> "Prone to wander, Lord, I feel it,
> Prone to leave the God I love;
> Here's my heart, Oh take and seal it,
> Seal it for thy courts above."

Many years ago someone, doubtless a sincere believer in Christian victory, proposed changing the first two lines to read

> "Prone to love thee, Lord, I feel it,
> Prove to serve the God I love."

However, I well remember how Dr. John R. Church, a Methodist evangelist known as a strong preacher of holiness, in a sermon in the Methodist Church in Wilmore, Kentucky, emphatically rejected the proposed change. He insisted that no matter how high our state of grace might be, we are always subject to failure if we become careless and fail to appropriate continually God's cleansing power.

As *The Christian's Secret*[21] so well points out, if we fail in this way it does not mean either that our experience of heart-cleansing was not real nor that we will now have to start over from the beginning. It means nothing more nor less than that we have failed to appropriate the grace God has made available to us for victory. *The remedy for failure is simply to admit that we have sinned, confess it to God, trust him for forgiveness, be warned by the experience, and get up and walk again in faith.*

How Do I Receive This Experience?

Entering into this experience is simple, from one point of view, but it may be as difficult as it was to admit that we were sinners and needed to let Jesus save us. I personally longed for this experience for a good while as a teenager, but with my feelings of insecurity I was unwilling to go to the church altar to pray for it unless the pastor or evangelist gave a specific invitation for this experience. After all, I reasoned (with Satan's help, of course!), I didn't want people to think that I was going to the altar to be converted! For other persons, as some of the testimonies we have mentioned have indicated, the problem is unwillingness to make a complete surrender to Jesus. For others, it may be a question of whether such an experience and life are really possible.

When the obstacles are dealt with, however, I think we can say that *to enter this experience is simple—simple acceptance by faith.* When we believe that God offers us this opportunity, and when we recognize that we need it, then we can simply ask God to cleanse our hearts and make us holy in his sight, believe that he does so, accept it by faith, and get on with living, trusting God for victory when the test comes. There may be an immediate emotional response in our heart, or there may be such a response later, or there may be nothing more than—but the "nothing more" is the important thing—nothing more than seeing how God's grace begins to work in our lives in the situations where we have previously encountered defeat.

How about you? If you are not experiencing the victory of heart purity and holiness, what do you have to lose? If our

---

[21] Chapter 11.

explanation of the Greek text is mistaken and if the experience of multitudes of Christians concerning this experience is mistaken, and if you surrender your life completely to God and ask him for this grace and he tells you, "Sorry, but I can't help you," you are no worse off than before except perhaps for a brief sense of disappointment. But if you meet the conditions we have mentioned and find that God *is* ready, willing, and able to give you this victory, as I know he is, then you will have the beginning of a life, not of "sinless perfection," but a life in which, as you let God's grace work by faith, you will find that victory is the norm and defeat is the exception.